2ND EDITION

PIANO
Adventures®
by Nancy and Randall Faber
THE BASIC PIANO METHOD

P9-DMW-783

This book belongs to: Srisha Vishwanath

Montclair Music Studio
104 Watchung Avenue
Upper Montclair, NJ 07043
973-783-4330

Special Thanks to our pilot teachers and consultants,
Lisa Studtmann and Barbara Anderson

Production: Jon Ophoff
Cover and Illustrations: Terpstra Design, San Francisco
Engraving: Dovetree Productions, Inc.
Consulting Editors: Barbara Anderson and Lisa Studtmann

ISBN 978-1-61677-078-5

Progress Chart

Keep track of your progress.
Color or put a star sticker for each item.

	Lesson	Theory	Technique	Performance	Sightreading
Get Ready for Take-off! (Primer Review)	4				
Head Start for Treble and Bass Clef Lines	6				
Firefly (Review piece)	8		2		6-9
UNIT 1 Legato and Staccato					
Little River (Legato Steps)	10	2	2, 4-5	2	
Sailing in the Sun	11	3			10-13
Ferris Wheel	12	4-5	6-7	3	
Mexican Jumping Beans	14	6	3, 8		
The Haunted Mouse	15	7	9	4-5	14-17
Classic Dance	16				18-21
Young Hunter	17	8-9	10-11	6-7	
UNIT 2 Treble F-A-C-E					
Skipping in Space	18	10	12		
Half-Time Show	19	11		8-9	22-25
The Lonely Pine	20	12	13		
Li'l Liza Jane	21	13			26-29
UNIT 3 Treble C-D-E-F-G on the Staff					
C's Rock!	22	14			
Mozart's Five Names	23	15			30-33
Paper Airplane	24	16	3, 14		
The Juggler	25	17	15	10-11	34-37
UNIT 4 Intervals (2nd, 3rd, 4th, 5th)					
Traffic Jam 2nds	26	18			
This is Not Jingle Bells	27		16	12	
Kites in the Sky	28	19		13	38-41
A Mixed-Up Song	30	20-21	17		42-45
Flute of the Andes	32			14	
Runaway Rabbit	33		18	15	46-49
Rain Forest	34	22-23	19		
Lightly Row	35	24-25	20-21	16-17	50-53

FF1078

Get Ready for Take-off!
(Primer Review)

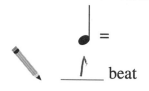
RHYTHM

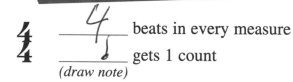 ♩ = __1__ beat   𝅗𝅥 = __2__ beats   𝅗𝅥. = __3__ beats   𝅝 = __4__ beats   𝄽 = __1__ beat

TIME SIGNATURES

$\frac{4}{4}$ __4__ beats in every measure
__♩__ *(draw note)* gets 1 count

$\frac{3}{4}$ __3__ beats in every measure
__♩__ *(draw note)* gets 1 count

DYNAMIC MARKS   Dynamics are the "louds and softs" in the music.

Circle the correct answer.

forte (𝒇) means   (**loud**) / **soft**

piano (𝒑) means   **loud** / (**soft**)

mezzo forte (𝒎𝒇) means   (**moderately loud** / **moderately soft**)

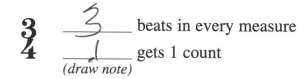
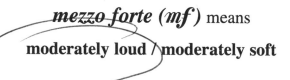

p   mp   mf   f

NOTE NAMES

Name the notes below.

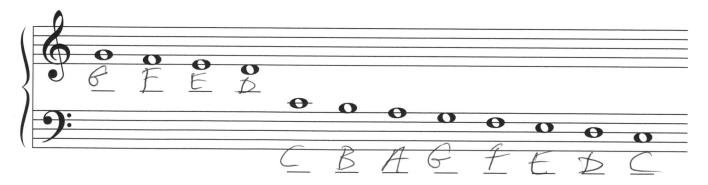

G F E D

C B A G F E D C

STEPS   Steps move from a **line to a space** or a **space to a line** on the staff.

Draw **steps** up or down:

step UP   step DOWN   step UP   step DOWN

SKIPS   Skips move from a **line to a line** or a **space to a space** on the staff.

Draw **skips** up or down:

skip DOWN   skip UP   skip DOWN   skip UP

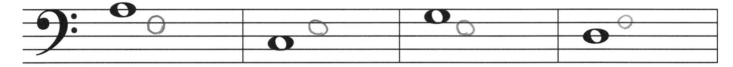

C 5-Finger Scale Warm-Up

Play hands alone and hands together.

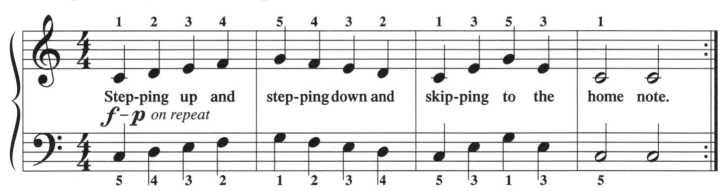

Preview: G 5-Finger Scale

Find the **G 5-finger scale** on the piano. G is now the "home note."
Play the scale warm-up above with the **G 5-finger scale**.

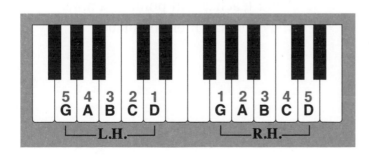

Head Start for Treble Clef Lines
The Adventures of E-G-B Mouse

Mouse Mission #1
Memorize and say my name quickly 3 times.

Mouse Mission #2
Play my name on the piano 3 times.

Mouse Mission #3
Your teacher will call for, "Line 1," or "Line 5," etc. How fast can you play and say the note?

Mouse Mission #4
Darken the notes so the letters disappear! Your teacher will point to a note. Play and say it on the piano.

Teacher Note: Do these reading activities throughout this level. Regular review will develop confident note readers.

FF1078

Head Start for Bass Clef Lines
3 Bass Clef "Smart Notes"

Mouse Mission #5
Your teacher will point to a "smart note."
How fast can you play and say it?

Mouse Mission #6
Are you ready to fly in the dark?
Darken the notes and try again.

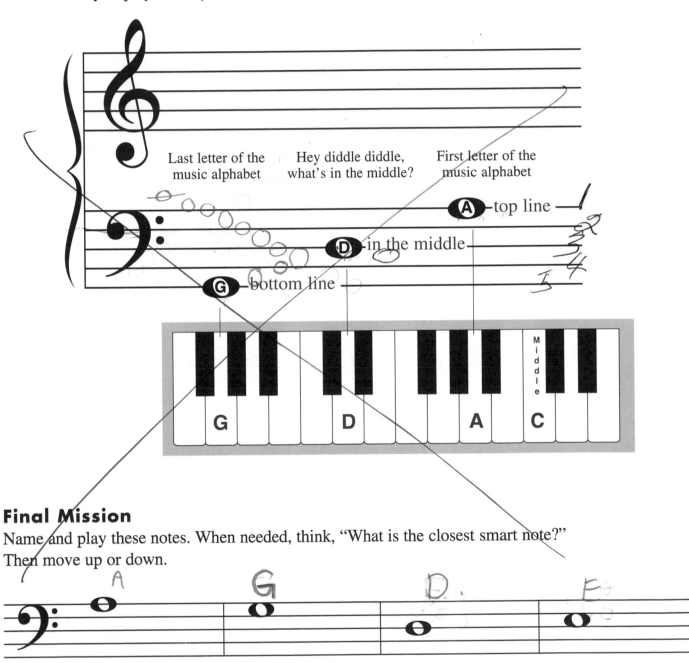

Last letter of the music alphabet

Hey diddle diddle, what's in the middle?

First letter of the music alphabet

A — top line

D — in the middle

G — bottom line

Final Mission
Name and play these notes. When needed, think, "What is the closest smart note?"
Then move up or down.

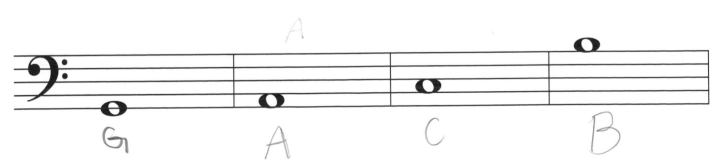

Review Piece

Circle the following symbols in *Firefly*.

- treble clef or G clef
  Trace the **G line** for measure 1.

- bass clef or F clef
  Trace the **F line** for measure 1.

- *mezzo forte* (**mf**)   *piano* (**p**)

- time signature

Firefly

C 5–Finger Scale

Moderately

5 *on* __?

mf Fire - fly,   fire - fly,   light - ing up the   eve - ning sky,

(prepare L.H.)

1 *on* __?

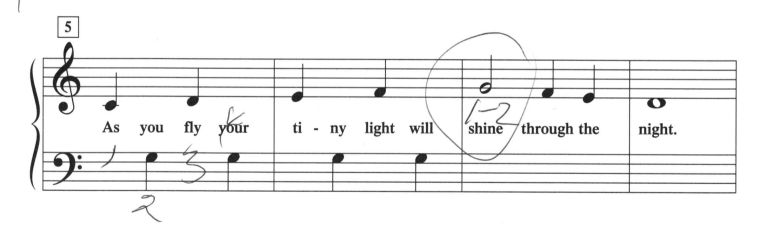

5

As you fly your   ti - ny light will   shine through the   night.

Teacher Duet: (Student plays *1 octave higher*)

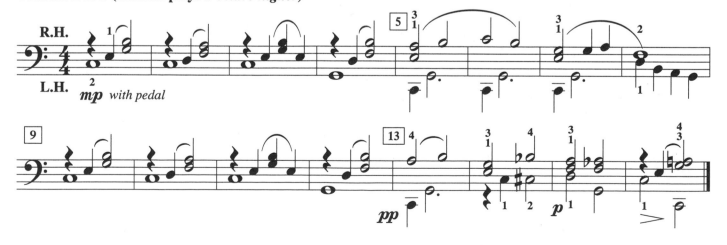

R.H.

L.H. **mp** *with pedal*

5

9

13

pp

p

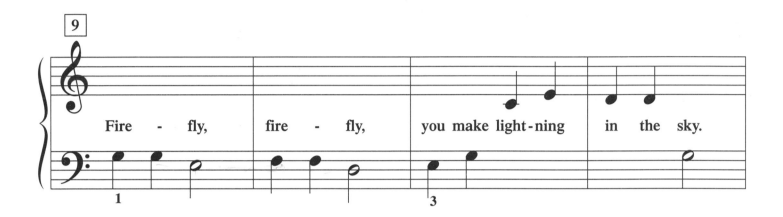

Fire - fly, fire - fly, you make light-ning in the sky.

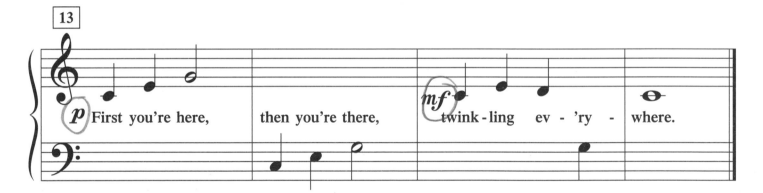

p First you're here, then you're there, *mf* twink-ling ev - 'ry - where.

Transposing

Did you know that you can play *Firefly* using the **G 5-finger scale**?

* Place hands in the G 5-finger scale. Read steps, skips, and repeats!

* This is called **transposing**. Say this word aloud with your teacher.

G 5-Finger Scale

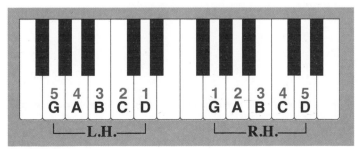

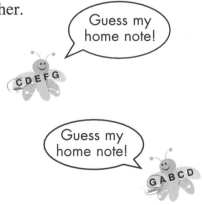

Guess my home note!

Guess my home note!

Legato — connect the notes, with no break in the sound.

When you walk, one foot goes down as the other foot comes up.
To play LEGATO, one finger goes down as the other finger comes up!

- On the closed keyboard lid, walk back and forth
  with **fingers 2** and **3**. Try this with each hand.

- Repeat this exercise with **fingers 1-2** and **3-4**.

Slur — a curved line over or under a group
of notes that means to play legato.

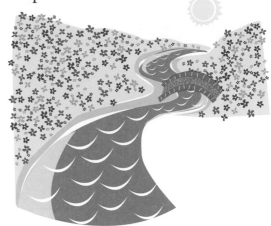

Little River
C 5-Finger Scale

Flowing smoothly

wrist float-off

1 *on __?*

mf

Lit - tle riv - er flow - ing un - der - neath the bridge.

5

Lit - tle riv - er flow - ing un - der - neath the bridge. *wrist float-off*

p

1 *on __?*

DISCOVERY

Can you transpose this piece to the **G 5-finger scale**?

Teacher Duet: (Student plays *1 octave higher*)

R.H.

L.H.
mp *ped. simile*

pp

Sailing in the Sun

Rhythm Check: Feel the quarter rests!

Briskly *FAST*

Words by Crystal Bowman

1 *on* __?

mf Come, go sail - ing | with me, | it's ex - cit - ing, | you'll see.

1 *on* __?

5

3

What a feel - ing, | so free, | when you're sail - ing | the sea!

9

3
1

4
2

p Feel the wind blow | in your hair | while the sun - shine | warms the air.
grow *louder* | | *f*

3

13

mf When you're sail - ing | on the o - cean, | life's the best it | can be!

DISCOVERY Find a one-measure slur, a very short slur, and a l-o-n-g slur.

CD 6-7 ✏ 3 ∿ 10-13

About the Damper Pedal

The **damper pedal** is the pedal on the right.

Pedal mark:

Pedal	*hold it down*	Pedal
DOWN		UP

Use your right foot for the damper pedal.
Your teacher will show you.

Ferris Wheel

Gracefully

Words by Crystal Bowman

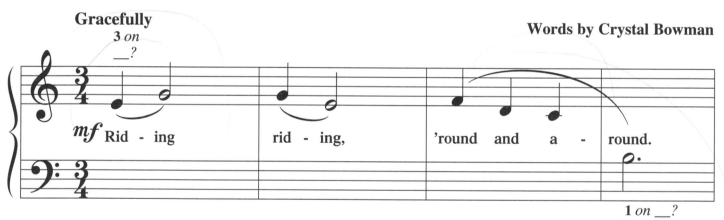

mf Rid - ing   rid - ing,   'round and a - round.

Turn - ing,   turn - ing,   down   to   the   ground.

Teacher Duet: (Student plays *1 octave higher*. Teacher pedals for duet.)

CD 8-9   4-5   6-7   3

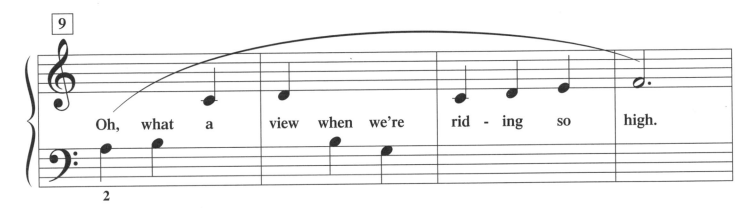

9

Oh, what a view when we're rid - ing so high.

2

13

I just love the fer - ris wheel ride.

3

3
1

3

Teacher Note: Teach by demonstration.

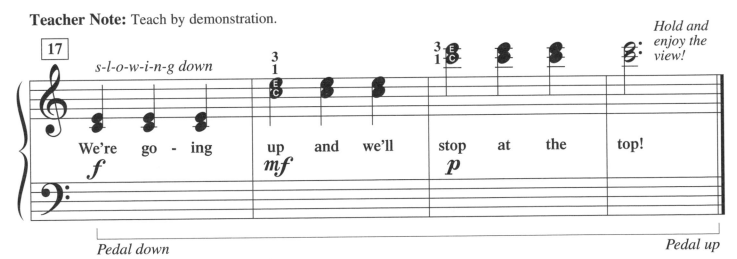

17

s-l-o-w-i-n-g down

We're go - ing up and we'll stop at the top!

f   *mf*   *p*

3
1
E
C

3
1
E
C

Hold and enjoy the view!

Pedal down   *Pedal up*

DISCOVERY Point out the **slur** that includes 4 measures.

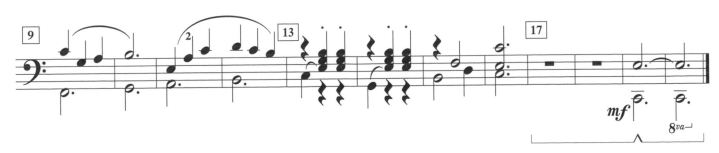

9   2   13   17

mf

8va

Staccato — separate the notes to create a crisp, detached sound.

To play staccato, quickly lift the finger off the key.
Staccato is the opposite of legato.

The staccato mark is a small dot placed
above or **below** the note.

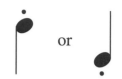 or

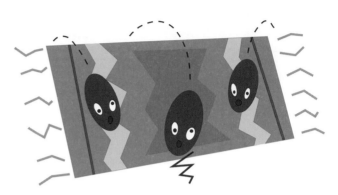

Warm-Ups

1. Brace finger 3's with the thumb to make an oval "bean shape." Play the song, hopping with finger 3's.

2. Now play with all five fingers. Listen for a crisp, *staccato* sound!

Mexican Jumping Beans
C 5-Finger Scale

Jumpy

Words by Crystal Bowman

1 on __?

p Beans are jump-ing | here and there, | jump-ing beans are | ev-'ry-where.

1 on __?

5

Play the highest C on the piano! **C**

Jump-ing left and | jump-ing right, | one bean just jumped | out of sight!

Teacher Duet: (Student plays *as written*)

R.H.

L.H. *p*

The Haunted Mouse

Finger Check: Are your fingers curved
and playing on their tips?

Scampering along

I'm a lit-tle mouse that's in a haunt-ed house.

I will al-ways squeak when I hear peo-ple shriek!

g-r-o-w   l-o-u-d-e-r

It's a lot of fun to watch the peo-ple run. Oh,

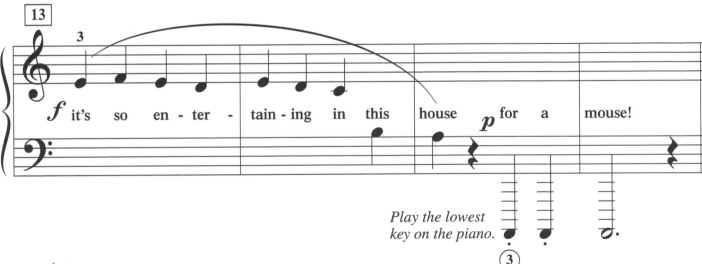

it's so en-ter-tain-ing in this house for a mouse!

*Play the lowest
key on the piano.*

DISCOVERY

Identify each curved line as a **slur** or a **tie**.

Warm-Up for Measure 3

- Play this measure *legato* three times.
  Notice the same fingers play together.

- Now play it *staccato* several times.
  Are your wrists relaxed as you play?

Classic Dance

5-Finger Scale

Repeat this line.

Rather quickly

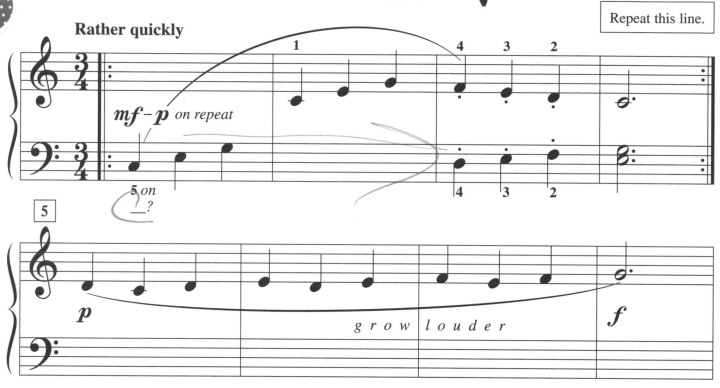

mf – p on repeat

5 *on*
___?

5

p

grow louder

f

9

mf

s-l-o-w | *down and get softer*

p

DISCOVERY

Does each measure *step* or *skip?* Now transpose to the **G 5-finger scale**.

Teacher Duet: (Student plays *as written*)

R.H.

L.H. *mf – p*

Fine

D.C. al Fine

Treble A

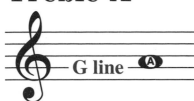

G line — **A**

This A is on **space 2**.
It is a step above the G line.

- Find this **A** on the keyboard.
- Play with R.H. fingers 2, 3, then 4.

Young Hunter

Words by Jennifer MacLean

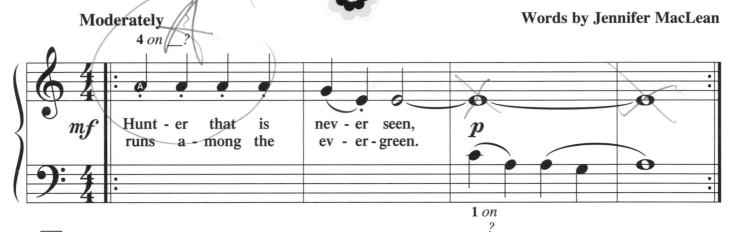

Moderately

4 *on* ___?

mf Hunt - er that is nev - er seen,
runs a - mong the ev - er - green.

p

1 *on*
___?

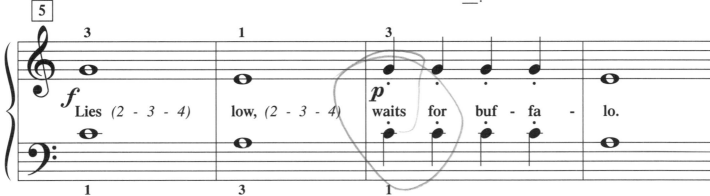

5

f Lies *(2 - 3 - 4)* low, *(2 - 3 - 4)* *p* waits for buf - fa - lo.

9

mf Lives be - side the rush - ing stream. *p*

D I S C O V E R Y

Which lines of music are the **same**? Can you memorize this piece?

Teacher Duet: (Student plays *1 octave higher*)

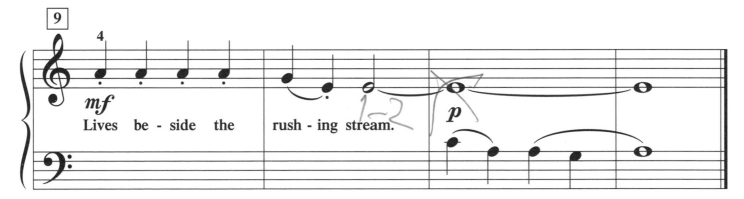

R.H.

L.H. *mf* *p* *p* *mf* Fine *p* D.C. al Fine

FACE the Treble Spaces

The space notes on the treble staff spell the word **FACE**.

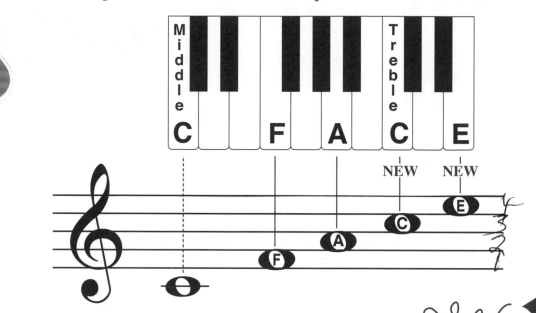

- Find the F key just above Middle C.
- Play and say the treble space notes F-A-C-E. Did you *step* or *skip?*

Skipping in Space

Steady

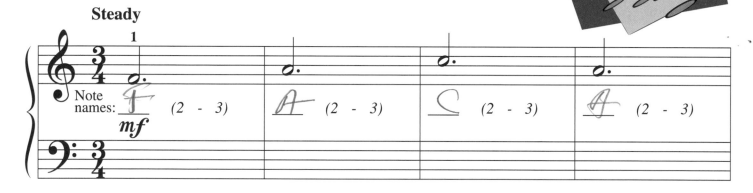

Note names: F (2 - 3)   A (2 - 3)   C (2 - 3)   A (2 - 3)

mf

Pedal down

5   *L.H. 2 crosses over to E*

F A C   F A C   F A C E

p

Pedal up

 CREATIVE

Can you play this piece with a L.H. cross-over to **F**? Cross-over to **A**? To **C**?

Half-Time Show

With energy   **1** *on*
___?

Up the field they come, (2 - 3 - 4) march-ing band at half - time.
Down the field they go, (2 - 3 - 4) march-ing band at half - time.

mf

1 *on* ___?

Hav - ing so much fun, (2 - 3 - 4) play - ing at the game.
What a mu - sic show, (2 - 3 - 4) for the foot - ball game!

repeat!

f RAH - RAH!   RAH - RAH!   We'll win the game! Hey!

DISCOVERY Can you transpose this piece a step higher to the **G 5-finger scale**?

Teacher Duet: (Student plays *as written*)

mp

mf

*Teacher Note: Stemming may be explained here,
but is formally introduced in the Theory Book, p. 15.

 CD 20-21   11   8   22-25   19

This piece uses a **hand shift** at *measure 6*.

- Trace the circled finger number as a reminder to shift your R.H. down.

The Lonely Pine

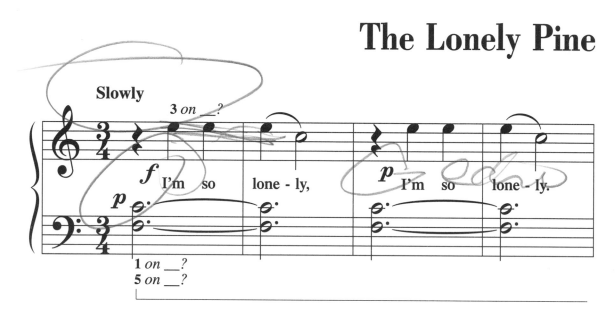

Slowly

3 *on* __?

f I'm so lone - ly, p I'm so lone - ly.

p

1 *on* __?
5 *on* __?

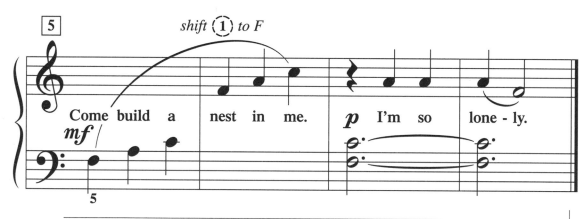

5 | shift (1) *to F*

Come build a nest in me. p I'm so lone - ly.

mf

5

C R E A T I V E

Draw a bird in the tree so that it's not so lonely.

Teacher Duet: (Student plays *as written*. Teacher pedals for duet.)

R.H.

3

L.H. mp 1 pp

5

mp 2 pp 1 3

mp 3 pp 5 pp 1 $8va$

CD 22-23 12 13

New Dynamic Mark

mp — **mezzo piano**
moderately soft

• Circle the *mp* marks below.

Li'l Liza Jane

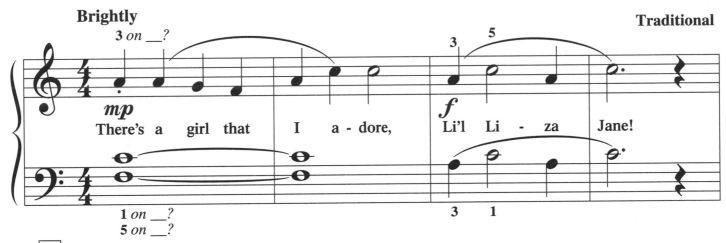

Brightly   Traditional

mp
There's a   girl that   I   a - dore, Li'l Li - za Jane!

f

5

mp
She's the one who   lives next door,   Li'l Li - za   Jane.

f

DISCOVERY Transpose *Li'l Liza Jane* a step higher to the **G 5-finger scale**.

Teacher Duet: (Student plays *1 octave higher*)

CD 24-25   13   26-29

Three C's on the Grand Staff

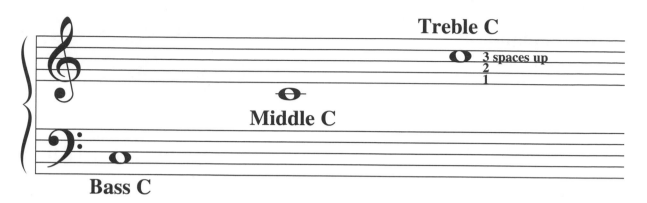

Treble C

3 spaces up
3
2
1

Middle C

Bass C

- **Play** and **say** the name of each C several times.

- Before playing, circle all the **Treble C's**.

C's Rock!

Fast rock beat

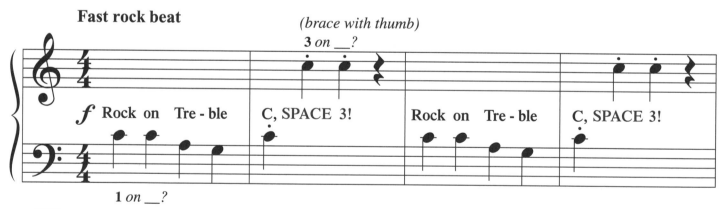

(brace with thumb)

3 on __?

𝆑 Rock on Tre - ble   C, SPACE 3!   Rock on Tre - ble   C, SPACE 3!

1 on __?

5

Leap   an   oc - tave.   Rock   on   Tre - ble   C, SPACE 3!

③

⑤   ①

DISCOVERY Can you play this piece with your L.H. thumb starting on **Bass C** (1 octave lower)?
Now play with your L.H. starting 2 octaves lower!

Treble C-D-E

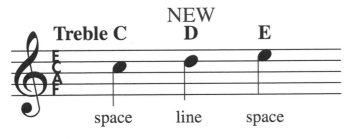

Treble C   **NEW** D   E

space   line   space

- Play and say these three notes.

Mozart's Five Names*

Wolfgang Amadeus Mozart
(1756-1791, Austria)
arranged

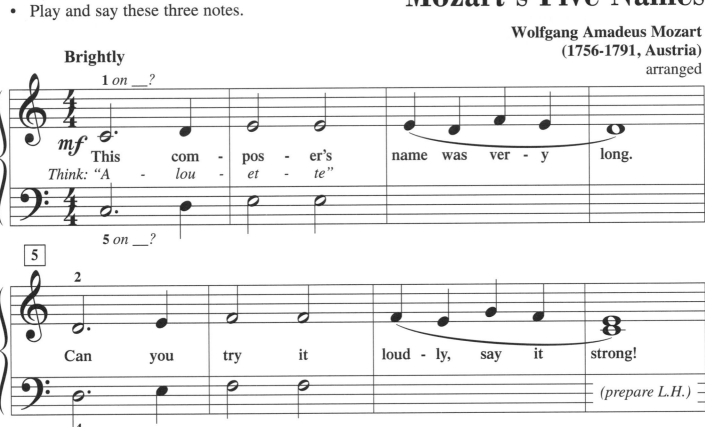

Brightly

1 on __?

mf

This com - pos - er's   name was ver - y   long.

Think: "A - lou - et - te"

5 on __?

5

2

Can   you   try   it   loud - ly,   say   it   strong!

(prepare L.H.)

4

9

5

Say, "Jo - han - nes   Chrys - os - to - mus   Wolf - gang   A - ma -

f

③

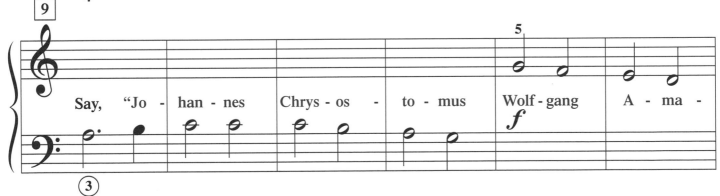

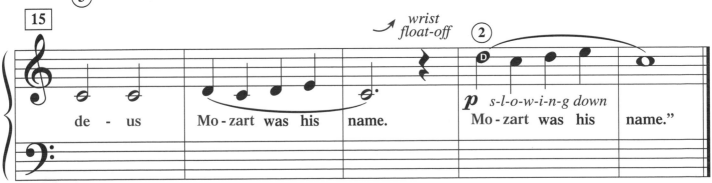

15

wrist float-off   **②**

de - us   Mo - zart was his   name.   Mo - zart was his   name."

p   *s-l-o-w-i-n-g down*

DISCOVERY   What is your full name?

From Quartet in C, KV157

Treble C-D-E-F-G

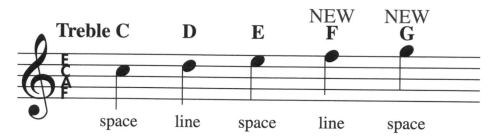

Treble C   D   E   **NEW** F   **NEW** G

space   line   space   line   space

- Play these five notes with R.H. fingers 1-2-3-4-5.
  Are you **stepping** or **skipping**?

Paper Airplane

Steady

1 *on* __?   steps or skips?   steps or skips?   steps or skips?

mf With a toss my   pa-per air-plane   takes to   flight.

5

5   steps or skips?   steps or skips?   steps or skips?

Will the wind then   take it high and   out of   sight?

(prepare L.H.)

9

steps or skips?   steps or skips?   steps or skips?

5

f Fly-ing   high!   *p* Now my air-plane's   glid-ing   down.

1 *on* __?

Teacher Duet: (Student plays *1 octave higher*)

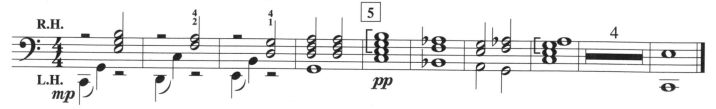

R.H.

mp   L.H.   *pp*

The Juggler

Brightly **3** *on* __?
  1 *on* __?

Ap - ples, peach-es, | pears, or grapes, | he can jug - gle | chi - na plates, or

mf

1 *on* __?

5

bowl - ing pins and | rub - ber balls. | He can toss them | all!

9 The juggler juggles C's!

1 *R.H. crosses over*

Throws   fast. | Spins 'round. | Noth-ing will | touch   ground.

mp *R.H.* ② *over*   *R.H.* ② *over*

1 *L.H.* 1 **1** *L.H.* 1

13

① *R.H. over*

Three C's fly - ing | in   the   air. | Try it if you | dare!

R.H. ② *over* *f*

1 *L.H.* 1 **2**

D I S C O V E R Y

Can you memorize this piece?

Naming Intervals

Interval of a 2nd

The distance between two notes on the keyboard or staff is an **interval**.

You have already learned the intervals of a **step** and a **skip**.
Now we will give them new names.

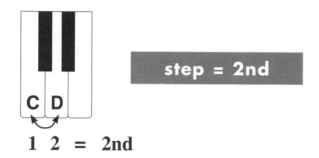

step = 2nd

1 2 = 2nd

2nds move to the **next letter** of the alphabet.

Traffic Jam 2nds

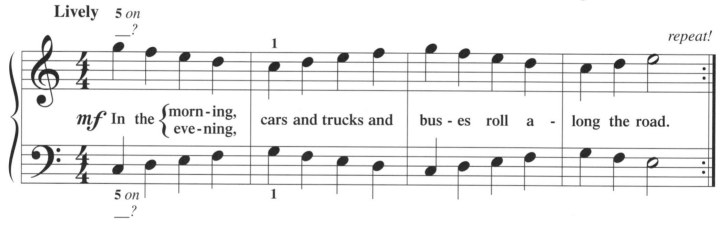

Lively **5** *on* ___?

repeat!

mf In the { morn-ing, eve-ning, } cars and trucks and bus-es roll a - long the road.

5 *on* ___?

5 **2** **1** *Notice how 2nds look and sound!*

f Honk-ing cars! | Honk-ing trucks! | On the road in | Rush Hour!

DISCOVERY

2nds move from a LINE to the next _____ or a SPACE to the next _____.

Interval of a 3rd

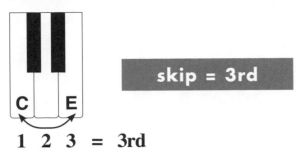

skip = 3rd

1 2 3 = 3rd

3rds **skip over a letter** of the alphabet.

YANKEE DOODLE AIR

This Is Not Jingle Bells

Happily

3 *on* __?
1 *on* __?   *Notice how 3rds look and sound!*

mp This is not   Jin - gle Bells.   Let me tell you   why.

1 *on* __?
3 *on* __?

f This is real - ly   Yan - kee Doo - dle   rid - ing on a   mo - tor - bike.

(prepare)

mp Could this be   Jin - gle Bells?   I don't know just   yet.

f Yan - kee Doo - dle   flew to Lon - don,   rid - ing on a   high - speed jet!

DISCOVERY

3rds move from a LINE to the next _____ or a SPACE to the next _____.

Listening Warm-Up

This piece has two sections.
Find each as your teacher demonstrates the piece.

- Which section uses **2nds**?
- Which section uses **3rds**?

Kites in the Sky

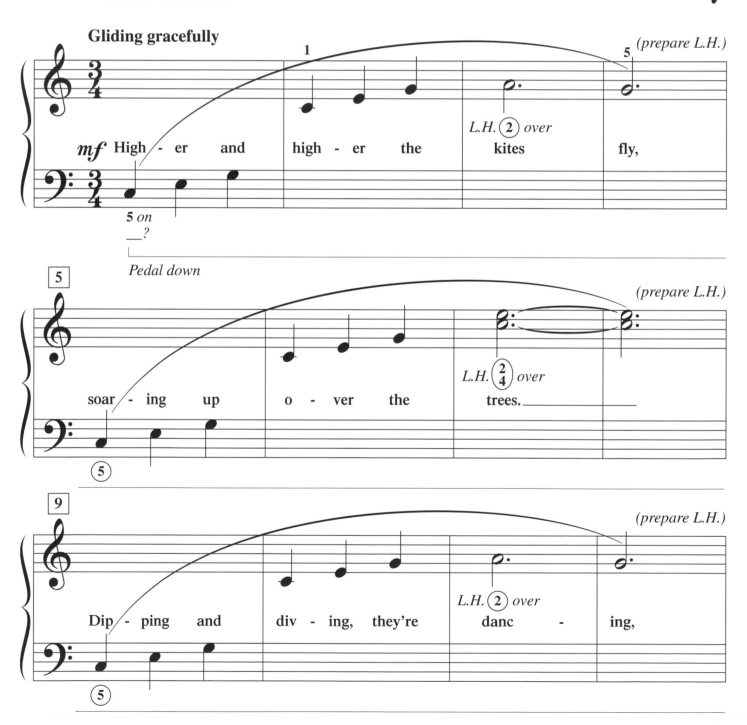

CD 38-39 ✏19 ✂13 ♫38-41   FF1078

13

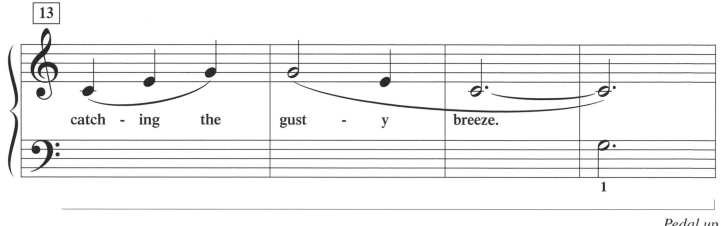

catch - ing   the   gust - y   breeze.

Pedal up

17 **Freely, climbing smoothly higher** (Your teacher will demonstrate.)

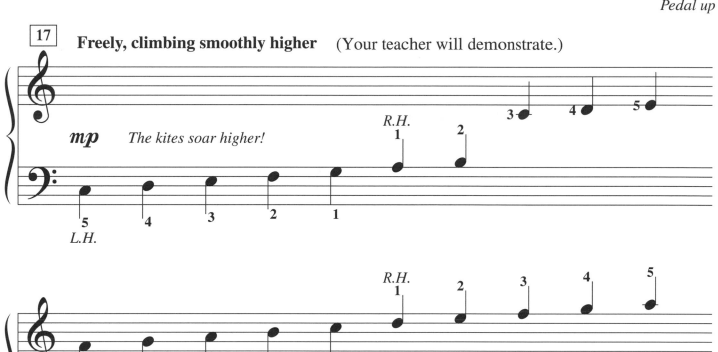

mp *The kites soar higher!*

R.H.

L.H.

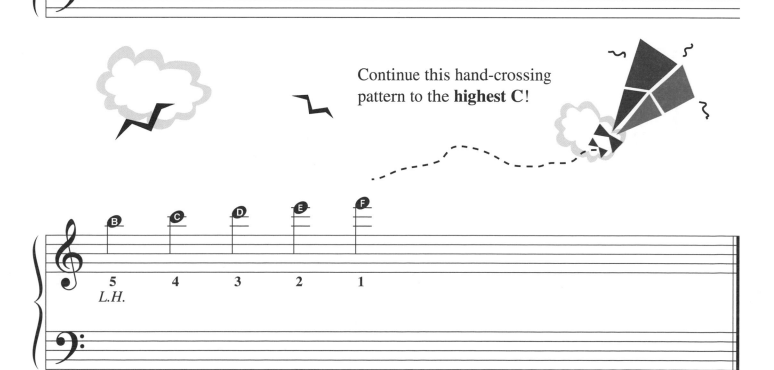

R.H.

L.H. over *s - l - o - w - i - n - g down*

Continue this hand-crossing pattern to the **highest C**!

L.H.

Interval of a 4th

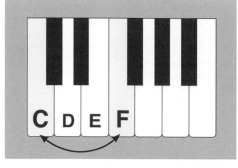

1 2 3 4 = 4th

A **4th** spans 4 letter names.

- Play a **C-F** fourth with R.H. fingers **1-4**.
  Does it sound like *Here Comes the Bride*?

- Repeat with L.H. using fingers **5-2**.

On the Staff

- Count each line and space, including the *first* and *last* note.
  Point to each number and count aloud.

line   to   a   space   or   space   to   a   line

A Mixed-Up Song

Fast and snappy

4 *on* __?
1 *on* __?

mf

2 *on* __?

5

1   4

f Once there was a   small   man,   thought he was a   tall   man,

fermata 𝄐 (fer-MAH-tah)
Hold this note longer than usual.

9
'cause he saw his shad - ow stretch - ing far and long.

13
mf

17
f Once there was a tall man, thought he was a small man,

21
'cause he saw his shad - ow, short and ver - y wide.

25
mf   *f*

DISCOVERY

a 4th DOWN from G is _____   a 4th UP from G is _____

Octave Sign $8^{va}-\rceil$

Play one octave higher than written.

Hold the damper pedal down throughout the piece.

Flute of the Andes

Moderately

1 *on* __?   4   *repeat!*

Sun - rise,   sun - set,   some-one's play - ing   a flute.
From the   moun - tains   some-one's play - ing   a flute.

mp   *mf*

4 *on*   1
__?

5

4

mf Can   you   hear   the   lit - tle wood - en   flute   play?

9

Sun - rise,   sun - set,   some - one's play - ing

mp   *mf*

4

12

$8^{va}----\rceil$

①

a   flute,   *mp* a   flute,   *p* a   flute.

DISCOVERY

Can you play this piece using **fingers 2-5** to play the 4th?

CD 42-43 with improv   14   FF1078

Runaway Rabbit

Quickly

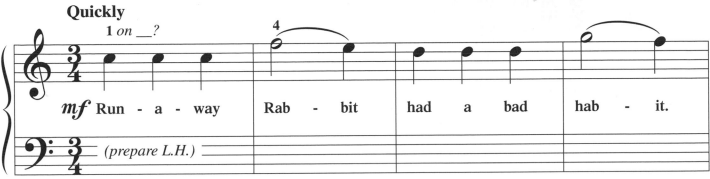

1 on __?

mf Run - a - way Rab - bit had a bad hab - it.

(prepare L.H.)

5

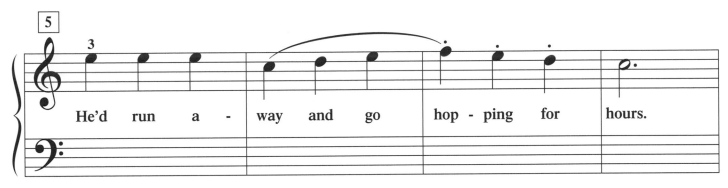

He'd run a - way and go hop - ping for hours.

9

We'd run be - hind him, then when we'd find him,

13

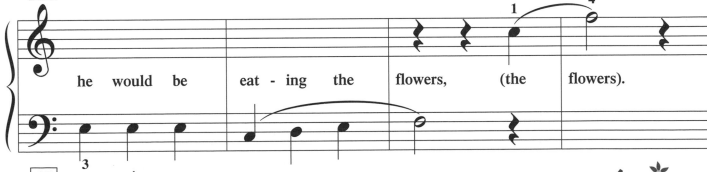

5 on __?

he would be eat - ing the flowers, (the flowers).

17

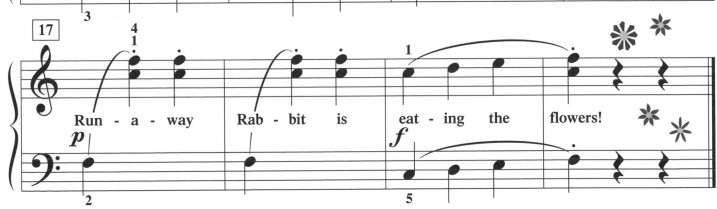

Run - a - way Rab - bit is eat - ing the flowers!

p   *f*

Interval of a 5th

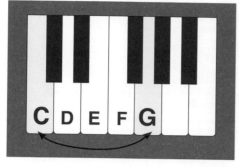

1 2 3 4 5 = 5th

A **5th** spans 5 letter names.

- Play a **C-G** fifth with R.H. fingers **1-5**.
  Does it sound like *Twinkle, Twinkle, Little Star?*

- Repeat with L.H. using fingers **5-1**.

On the Staff

- Count each line and space, including the *first* and *last* note.
  Point to each number and count aloud.

line   to   a   line   or   space   to   a   space

Rain Forest

Moving gently

(Begin the round.)

mp

1 - 2 - 3 - 4   1 - 2 - 3 - 4

mf

s-l-o-w-i-n-g down   *mp*

CREATIVE Play as a **round**. Student plays 1 octave higher. Teacher plays 1 octave lower and begins at *measure 3*.

Lightly Row

_____ **5-Finger Scale**

Finger Check: Are your fingers gently curved and playing on their tips?

Splashing happily

Traditional

5 on __?

mp Light - ly row, light - ly row, o - ver all the waves we go.

1 on __?
5 on __?

5 Sing and float, let's sing and float, we're in our lit - tle boat.

9 **p** Rock - ing, laugh - ing in the sun, sing - ing songs with ev - 'ry - one.

13 Light - ly row, let's **mp** light - ly row, we're in our lit - tle boat.

DISCOVERY Name each L.H. interval. Can you transpose to the **G 5-finger scale**?

Half Rest and Whole Rest

The half rest sits
above line 3 on the staff.

$=$ 2 beats of silence.

The whole rest hangs
below line 4 on the staff.

$=$ 4 beats of silence, or rest for any *whole* measure.

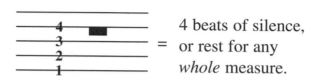

Forest Drums

Moving quickly (♩ = 144-160)

p *(1 - 2   half rest)*   *(1 - 2   half rest)*   *g r o w i n g   l o u d e r*

1 *on* __?
5 *on* __?

5

3 *on* __?

mf The for - est   calls to me,   I hear its   song. *(2 - 3 - 4)*

1
5

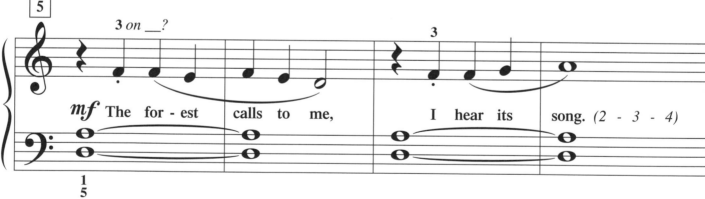

9

5

The sound of   rus - tling leaves, the   riv - er   strong. *(2 - 3 - 4)*

4

DISCOVERY

Name each **rest** in *measures 13-16*.

Now turn to *Lightly Row* on p. 35. Add a whole rest for the L.H. in each blank measure.

No Moon Tonight

Smoothly moving

No moon to - night,___

5

no moon to - night.___

9

Still - ness   fills   the   dark   eve - ning   sky,

13

no moon to - night.___

Teacher Duet: (Student plays *1 octave higher*)

pp-p on repeat
with pedal

Grumpy Old Troll

___ 5-Finger Scale

Poking along

4 on
___?

f Grump-y troll, grump-y troll, grump-y old troll grump-ing for his

1 on ___?
4 on ___?

5

2
1

p **f** hat! *Where is it?* *Where is it?* **p** *Where is my* **f** hat! *Drat!*

9

f Grump-y troll, grump-y troll, lost his hat and did not take his

13

nap! *Not sleep-y!* *Not sleep-y!* *YAWN!* *Snore,* *snore,* *snore!*
p (1-2-3-4)

5   2

15ᵐᵃ – – – – – – – – – – ⌐
(2 octaves lower)

CREATIVE Should the "snores" at the end be **f** or **p**?
Write your choice in the troll's missing hat.

Half Steps — From one key to the very next key is a **half step**.

1. Find and play these **half steps** on the piano.

Sharp ♯ — A sharp means to play the key a half step HIGHER.

2. Find and play these sharps on the piano.

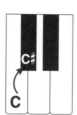 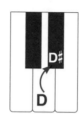 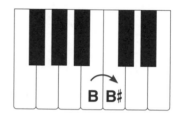

B sharp is a white key!
E sharp is also a white key.

Rule for Sharps

A sharp carries through a measure, but *not* past a bar line. In a new measure, the sharp must be written again.

still F♯

Merlin's Wand

Mysteriously

f Deep in the | for - est, now | flash goes his | wand! | *f*
p Mer - lin ap - | pears, now | Mer - lin is | gone! | POOF!

5 *on* ___?   **2** *still F♯*

Play the LOWEST C!

DISCOVERY Walk your fingers "into the forest" (toward the fallboard) to play the F♯'s.
Your wrist will rise slightly.

FF1078

Russian Sailor Dance

**Traditional
Russian Folk Song**

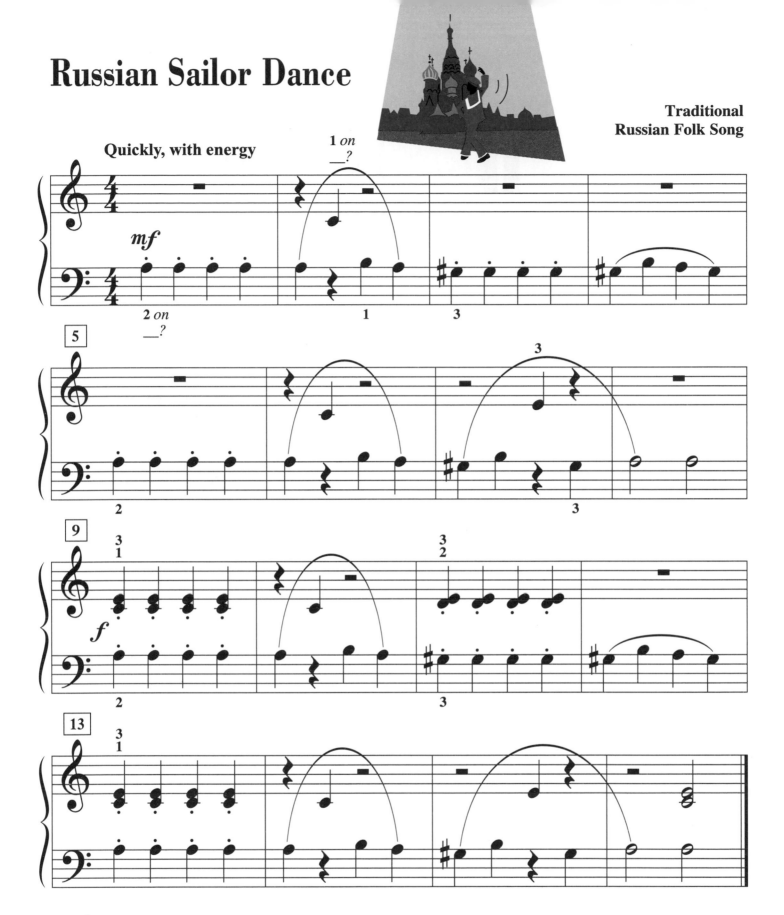

For a special ending, let the Russian sailor dance up and down the keyboard.
Use only A's and G♯'s in different octaves. End with the lowest A on the piano!

Teacher Duet: (Student plays *1 octave higher*)

mp – mf on repeat

CD 58-59   20-21   62-65

Flat ♭ — A flat means to play the key that is a **half step LOWER**.

1. Find and play these flats on the piano.

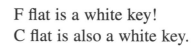

2. Your teacher will call for any flat. Play that key on the piano.

F flat is a white key!
C flat is also a white key.

Rule for Flats

A flat carries through a measure, but *not* past a bar line. In a new measure, the flat must be written again.

still E♭

Super Secret Agent

Slowly

f-p on repeat

still B♭

DISCOVERY Your teacher will play a black key. Can you say both its **flat** and **sharp** name?

Teacher Duet: (Student plays *as written*)

FF1078

Party Song

Learn *measures 5-6* first. Have fun
with the L.H. cross-over to A♭!

Words by Crystal Bowman

Brightly

I like go-ing to a par-ty. I like hav-ing fun.

Win-ning priz-es, play-ing games, fun for ev-'ry-one.

I am in the mood for some par-ty food.

I like go-ing to a par-ty. I like hav-ing fun.

CHALLENGE SECTION
You and your teacher may explore new **5-finger scales** that use *sharps and flats* on page 62.

Boogie on Broadway

Watch for the sharps and flats!

DISCOVERY Where are the first 2 measures found later in the piece? Circle them.

Teacher Duet: (Student plays *1 octave higher*)

CD 64-65 33 27

Find the Keys

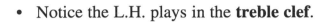

5 — L.H. — 1 1 2 3 4 5 — R.H.

Scarf Dance

Mauro Giuliani
(1781–1829, Italy)
adapted from Op. 50, No. 1

- Notice the L.H. plays in the **treble clef**.

Rather fast

1 on __?

Bel - la,* bel - la hear the gui - tar.

ƒ-p on repeat

1 on __?
5 on __?

5

Bel - la, bel - la mu - sic.

9

Wave the scarf, 'round and a - round.

ƒ-p on repeat

Repeat from measure 9 playing softly (**p**).

13

Bel - la, bel - la mu - sic.

DISCOVERY What note is flatted throughout the entire piece? _____

Bella is the Italian word for beautiful.

Tonic and Dominant

- In the C 5-finger scale, play FIRST note **C** and FIFTH note **G**.
  These are the two most important notes in the scale.

- Look at the descriptions for each note below.
  Learn **tonic** and **dominant**.

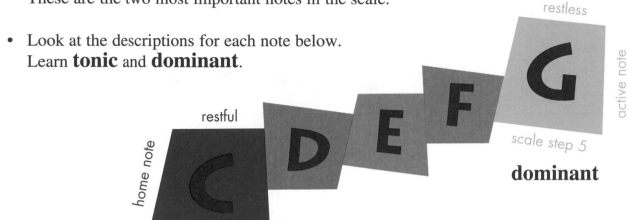

restless

restful

home note

active note

scale step 5

dominant

scale step 1

tonic

Two-Note March

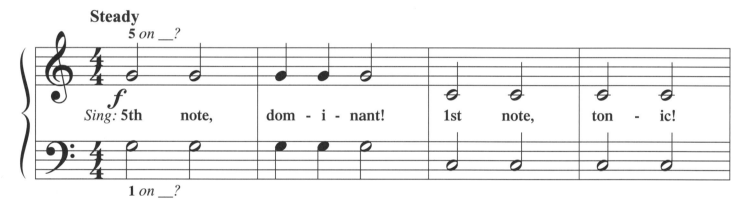

Steady

5 *on* __?

Sing: 5th note, dom - i - nant! 1st note, ton - ic!

1 *on* __?

5

Dom - i - nant, ton - ic, G back to C.

- Circle **tonic** or **dominant** for each measure. ✎

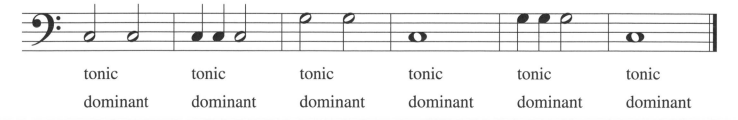

tonic   tonic   tonic   tonic   tonic   tonic

dominant   dominant   dominant   dominant   dominant   dominant

Girl on a Bicycle

Wheeling along

Music by Ferdinand Beyer
(1803-1863, Germany)
adapted

mf Rid - ing up and | down the hills, I | know I will not | take a spill. I

zoom a - round my | neigh - bor - hood each | day when school is | done!

DISCOVERY Identify each L.H. note as **tonic** or **dominant notes** in *measures 1-4*.

Boy on a Bicycle

Music by Ferdinand Beyer
adapted

Pedaling along

mf Cy - cling is my | fa - v'rite sport, I | e - ven did a | school re - port a -

bout my ten - speed | bi - cy - cle and | how I love to | ride!

DISCOVERY Pieces usually end on the **tonic**. Do both of these songs end on the tonic?

The C Chord

The C chord is made up of 3 tones that build up in **3rds** from C.

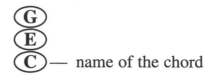

Ⓖ
Ⓔ
Ⓒ — name of the chord

Warm-Ups

1.   *mf*   *Repeat 8va higher.*

2.   *mf*   *Repeat 8va lower.*

Blocked Chord Study
(notes played at the same time)

Steady

5 *on* __?
3 *on* __?
1 *on* __?

f Chords march-ing,   Hup - 2 - 3 - 4!   *p* Chords march-ing   home, 2 - 3 - 4!

1 *on* __?
3 *on* __?
5 *on* __?

Broken Chord Study
(notes played separately)

Playfully

1   *L.H.* ② *over*

Roll-ing and   roll-ing, my   fin-gers are   roll-ing a - round like a   dol-phin at   sea.

mp

5 *on* __?

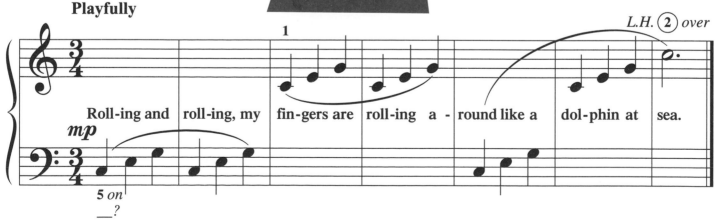

D I S C O V E R Y

Can you play these songs using a **G chord**? Hint: G will be the *lowest* note.

The I Chord

I is the Roman numeral for the number **1**.

The C chord is called the **I chord** in the C 5-finger scale.

tonic or home note

I

Warm-Up

Before playing this piece, write a **I** under each measure with a C chord.

Song for a Scarecrow

Words by Crystal Bowman

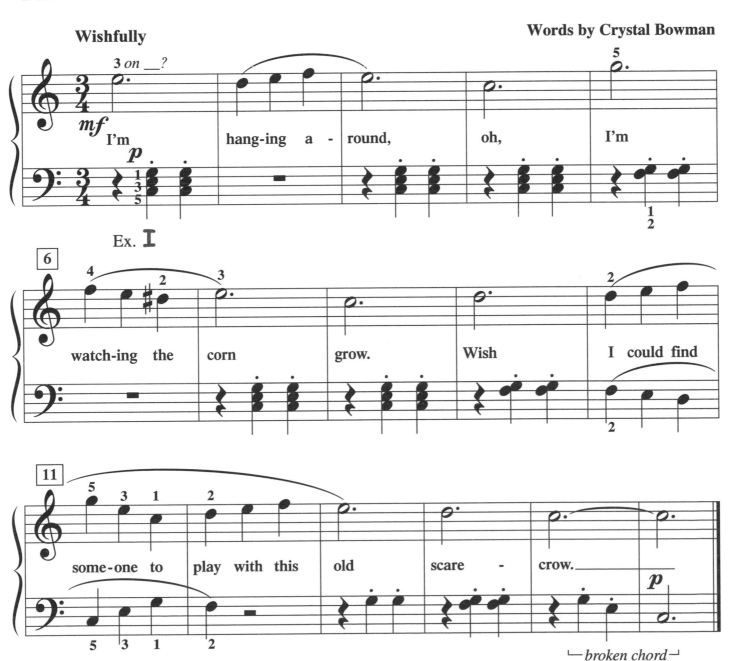

Wishfully

3 *on __?*

mf

I'm hang-ing a - round, oh, I'm

p

Ex. **I**

6

watch-ing the corn grow. Wish I could find

11

some-one to play with this old scare - crow._____

p

└─ *broken chord* ┘

- Write a **I** under each measure with a C chord.

My Pony

Trotting along

Traditional

mf Trot, trot, trot, go and nev - er stop!

Ex. **I**

Where it's smooth and where it's ston - y, go a - long my lit - tle po - ny.

p

①

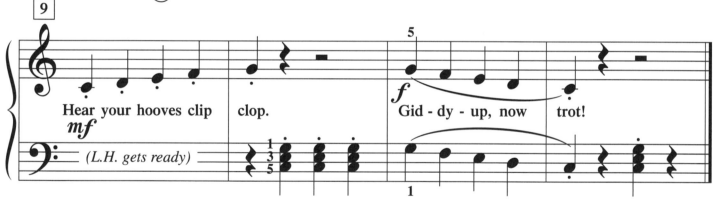

Hear your hooves clip clop. Gid - dy - up, now trot!

mf (L.H. gets ready) *f*

CREATIVE Hold the pedal down and play C chords beginning *high* and ending *low*.

Teacher Duet: (Student plays *1 octave higher*)

R.H.

L.H. *mp*

pp *mp* *mf*

CD 76-77   28-29   74-77

Row, Row, Row Your Boat

Fast

Traditional

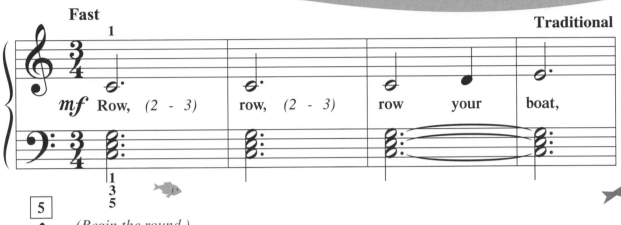

mf Row, (2 - 3) row, (2 - 3) row your boat,

5

(Begin the round.)

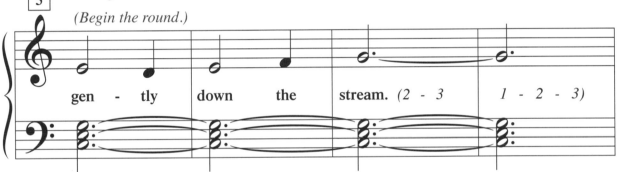

gen - tly down the stream. (2 - 3 1 - 2 - 3)

9 *L.H. over* ② *R.H.* 5 3

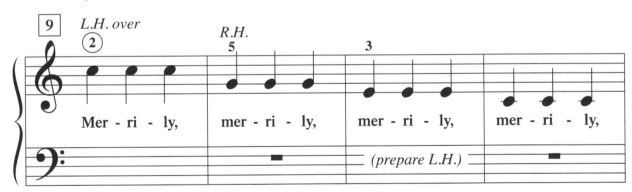

Mer - ri - ly, mer - ri - ly, mer - ri - ly, mer - ri - ly,

(prepare L.H.)

13 5

life is but a dream. *p*

DISCOVERY Play *Row, Row, Row Your Boat* as a round with your teacher. Teacher plays two octaves higher than written and begins at *measure 5*. Play two times.

The V⁷ Chord

V is the Roman numeral for the number **5**.

The **V⁷ chord** (pronounced "five-seven") is a 4-note chord.

(F) (D) (B) (G)

In this book, a simplified 2-note version of the V⁷ chord is used.

(F) (G) ← the dominant, **step V**

← F is **7 notes** above G. It is played just below G for ease.

V⁷

• Play the chords below and say their names aloud.

Play:
L.H.

I   V7   I

Play:
R.H.

I   V7   I

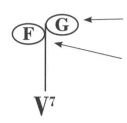

Theme from the

"London" Symphony

Franz Joseph Haydn
(1732-1809, Austria)
arranged

With spirit

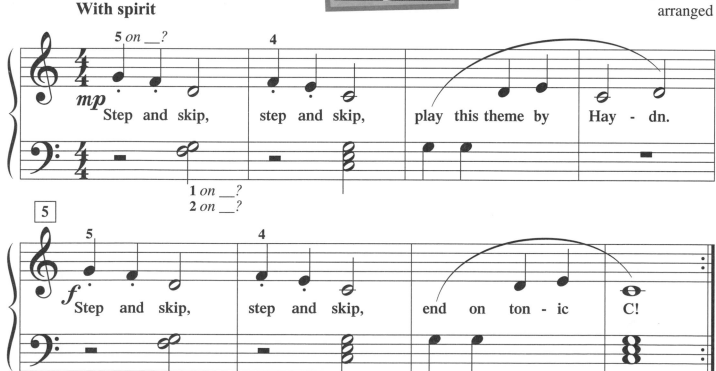

5 *on* __?

4

mp Step and skip,   step and skip,   play this theme by   Hay - dn.

1 *on* __?
2 *on* __?

5

5

4

f Step and skip,   step and skip,   end on ton - ic   C!

DISCOVERY

Write **I** or **V⁷** under each chord. ✏

Warm-Up

Identify each chord as a **I** or **V⁷** chord.

Jazzy Joe

Lively

1

mf There goes that Jazz - y Joe in his new fan - cy clothes.
He can play an - y - thing, rock 'n' roll, pop,___ or swing.

1
3
5

5

Ev - 'ry - one seems___ to know that Jazz - y Joe.
Ev - 'ry - one loves___ to sing with Jazz - y Joe.

1
2

9

(move R.H. quickly)

f La la la la___ la la, La la la la___ la la,

13

1

La la la la___ la la, **2** that Jazz - y Joe.___

Reading Chord Symbols

Place your hands in the C 5-finger scale. Play **I** and **V⁷** chords using these chord symbols.

Use L.H.: **I V⁷ I V⁷ I**   Use R.H.: **I I V⁷ V⁷ I**

CD 82-83   32   32-33

rit. = *ritardando*

This means a gradual slowing down of the speed of the music.
Ritardando is often shortened to *ritard.* or *rit.*

- Say this word with your teacher.

- Play the last line and practice the *ritardando*.

Shepherd's Song

(from the *Sixth Symphony*)

Ludwig van Beethoven
(1770–1827, Germany)
arranged

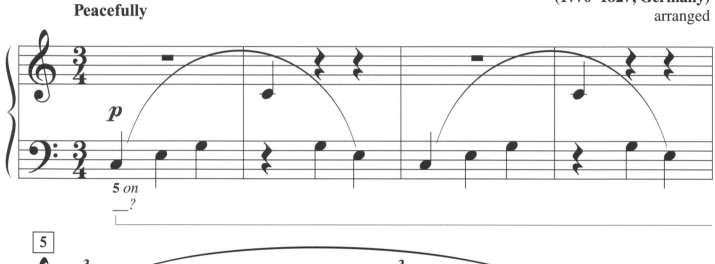

Peacefully

p

5 *on* __?

mp Bee - tho - ven's theme is a

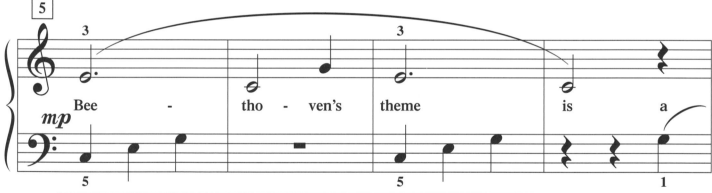

Teacher Duet: (Student plays *1 octave higher*)

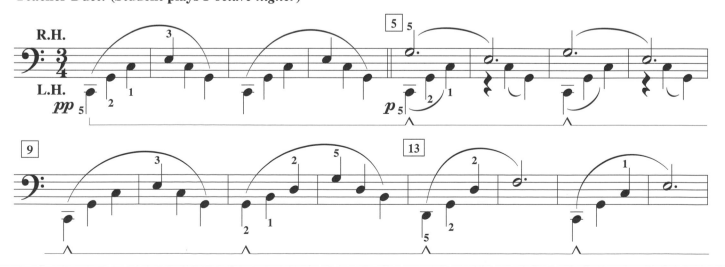

R.H.

L.H.
pp

p

CD 84-85   40-41   33   82-85

FF1078

DISCOVERY This piece has an *introduction* and *ending* section. Find these for your teacher.
What **broken chord** is used to create a peaceful sound? _____

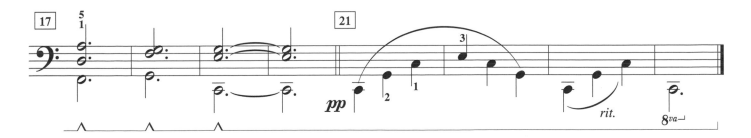

UNIT 10

Three G's on the Grand Staff

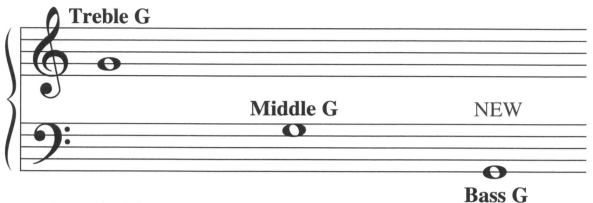

Treble G

Middle G   NEW

Bass G

- Play each of these G's and say its name aloud.

Bongo Drummers

Fast and rhythmic

Teacher Duet: (Student plays *as written*)

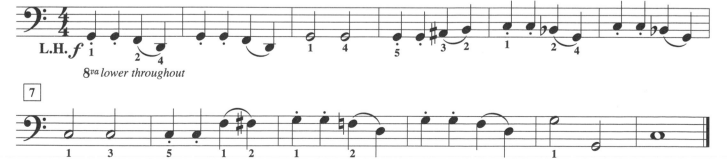

CD 86-87   42   FF1078

G 5-Finger Scales

Treble G

Bass G **Middle G**

- Play each **G 5-finger scale** above. Read by *steps*.

  The **tonic** (first note) is **G**.
  The **dominant** (fifth note) is **D**.

dominant

tonic

Warm-Up in G

Steady 1 *on* ___?

Ton - ic up to | dom - i - nant. | Ton - ic up to | dom - i - nant.

mf

5 *on* ___?

5

Play - ing sec - onds | in the G scale, | now play thirds with | ease.

5 *on* ___?

Chords in G

Smoothly

mp *broken chords* *blocked chords*

$\frac{5}{4}$ $\frac{1}{2}$

I   I   V^7 I

Accent Mark

Accent Mark ♩ or ♩ means accent the note by playing it louder than the others around it.

Dinosaur Stomp

_____ 5-Finger Scale

Slow and heavy

(prepare R.H.)

_f_ Crash! Boom! Thunk! Make way. Crash! Boom! Thunk! Love to

roar and do my pre-his-tor-ic danc-ing. All the

tree trunks break. The earth cracks and shakes. Love to

roar and do the Di-no-saur Stomp!

D I S C O V E R Y Is the first note in _measure 15_ the tonic or the dominant?
Does the piece end on the tonic or the dominant?

CD 88-89 44-45 36 34-37 86-89 FF1078

Upbeat

This piece begins with an **upbeat** (or **pick-up note**). The upbeat leads into the first full measure.

If a piece has an *upbeat,* the last measure will often be incomplete. The combined beats of the incomplete first and last measures will equal one full measure.

This piece begins on beat 4.

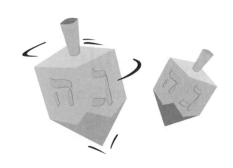

The Dreydl Song
_____ 5-Finger Scale

Traditional

CD 90-91   46   37

The Bubble

_____ 5-Finger Scale

Eye Check: Can you play this entire piece, except the last measure, without looking at your hands?

With excitement

Words by Crystal Bowman

I blew a great big bub-ble while chew-ing gum to - day. It

stretched out wide be - fore it popped, I'm real - ly pleased to say.

mp Gum got on my cheeks, and in my nose and hair.

mf Ev - ery-thing was look - ing pink but oh, I did - n't care. My

CD 92-93 47-48 38-39 38-40 90-95

FF1078

17

ears were plugged a lit - tle, some gum was on my chin. The

21

col - lar of my new white shirt was stick - ing to my skin. The

25

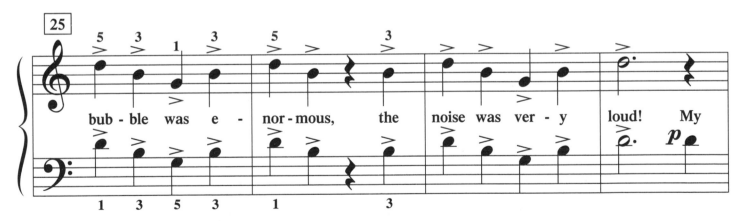

bub - ble was e - nor - mous, the noise was ver - y loud! My

29 **Very slowly**

Quickly

moth - er was - n't hap - py, but I was real - ly proud!

DISCOVERY

Which line of music uses only notes of the **G chord**? _____

Teacher Note: D and A 5-Finger Scales are introduced with notation at Level 2A. Students will benefit from learning these keyboard patterns away from the staff at Level 1.

For Adventurers

Explore some or all of these scales with your teacher.

- Use the **Adventure Warm-Up** on p. 63 for each scale.

- Transpose pieces from the book to these adventurous keys.

Think: Vanilla Cookie with Chocolate in the Middle

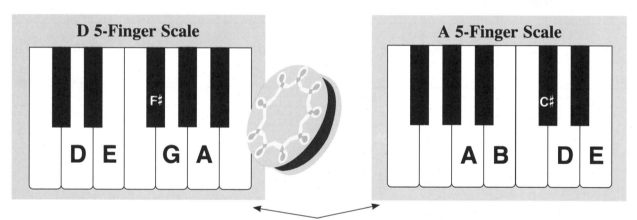

D 5-Finger Scale

F#

D E G A

A 5-Finger Scale

C#

A B D E

Why are these scales the "twins"?

Yum! Double Chocolate

E 5-Finger Scale

F# G#

E A B

Who Moved the Chocolate?

F 5-Finger Scale

B♭

F G A C

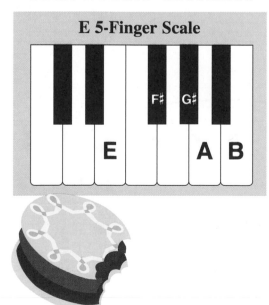

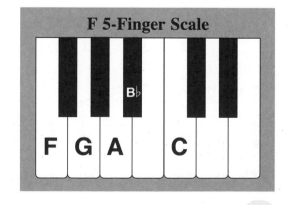

FF1078

Adventure Warm-Up in C

Adventure Warm-Up in G

Adventure Warm-Up with More Scales

Play the Adventure Warm-Up using the scales you have learned:

 C D E F G A

Piano Adventures® Certificate

Congratulations to:

_____

You have completed LEVEL 1

and are now ready for LEVEL 2A

LESSON BOOK   **THEORY BOOK**   **TECHNIQUE & ARTISTRY**   **PERFORMANCE BOOK**

Teacher:_____

Date:_____